Playtime with Music

FOR ANYONE WHO IS
OR EVER WAS
A CHILD

LYRICS AND TEXT BY
MARION ABESON

MUSIC AND ARRANGEMENTS BY
CHARITY BAILEY
MUSIC DIRECTOR, LITTLE RED SCHOOL HOUSE

ILLUSTRATIONS BY
SALLY MICHEL

WITH A POSTSCRIPT BY THE AUTHOR AND COMPOSER

COPYRIGHT, 1952, BY
LIVERIGHT PUBLISHING CORPORATION
NEW YORK

LIBRARY OF CONGRESS CATALOG CARD NUMBER: 52-7594

CONTENTS

WHO WANTS A RIDE?

IN

MY LITTLE RED WAGON

YOU ROLL ALONG,

THE TUGBOAT AND THE FREIGHTER

CHUG ALONG.

TAKE

A TUMBLY HAYRIDE,

TUMBLE IN THE HAY.

GALLOPING TO GRANDMA'S

YOU

GALLOP ALL THE WAY.

SING A SONG
AND RIDE ALONG.
WHERE SHALL WE RIDE TODAY?

MY LITTLE RED WAGON

LYRICS BY MARION ABESON

MUSIC BY CHARITY BAILEY

MY LITTLE RED WAGON

WHEN I WANT A RIDE
AND I HAVEN'T ANY FARE
MY LITTLE RED WAGON
RIDES ME EVERYWHERE.

RIDE ON A TUGBOAT

CHUG AND TUG WITH ME.

PULL IN A FREIGHTER

HOME FROM THE SEA.

THE TUGBOAT AND THE FREIGHTER

LYRICS BY MARION ABESON

MUSIC BY CHARITY BAILEY

A TUMBLY HAYRIDE

WOULD YOU LIKE A RIDE

WHERE YOU TUMBLE AND SLIDE?

THEN COME TO MY FARM

FOR A TUMBLY HAYRIDE:

LOAD SWEET HAY

ON A SUNNY DAY —

LOAD UP A WAGON

AND RIDE AWAY.

A TUMBLY HAYRIDE

LYRICS BY MARION ABESON

Folk Tune
ADAPTED BY MARION ABESON
ARRANGED BY CHARITY BAILEY

Fast and Gay

GOT MY-SELF TWO HOR-SES; GOT MY-SELF A WA-GON; NOW WE'LL FILL IT FULL OF HAY - O.
IF YOU'RE NOT TOO BU-SY, COME A-LONG, GET DIZ-ZY, TUM-BLING ON A LOAD OF HAY - O.

THEN I HITCH MY HOR-SES, JUMP UP ON THE WA-GON, TAKE THE REINS AND DRIVE A- WAY - O.
DRIV-ING TWO BIG HOR-SES, SIT-TING ON A WA-GON, RID-ING ON A LOAD OF HAY - O.

THIS WAY YOU TUM-BLE, THAT WAY YOU TUM-BLE, UP ON A LOAD OF HAY - O;

THIS WAY YOU TUM-BLE, THAT WAY YOU TUM-BLE, UP ON A LOAD OF HAY - O.

GALLOPING TO GRANDMA'S

LYRICS BY MARION ABESON

MUSIC BY CHARITY BAILEY

LOOK AT THOSE PONIES
PAWING THE GROUND
WAVING THEIR TAILS
AND PRANCING AROUND.
LET'S GO FOR A RIDE
TO GRANDMA'S TODAY —
LET'S JUMP ON OUR PONIES
AND

GALLOP

AWAY.

LET'S PLAY ZOO

LET'S ALL DO
WHAT
THE KANGAROO

THE SHINY BLACK SEAL

AND

THE MONKEY
DO.

LET'S CLUMP LIKE
THE RUMBLY ELEPHANT
TOO.

COME ON, EVERYBODY,
LET'S PLAY ZOO!

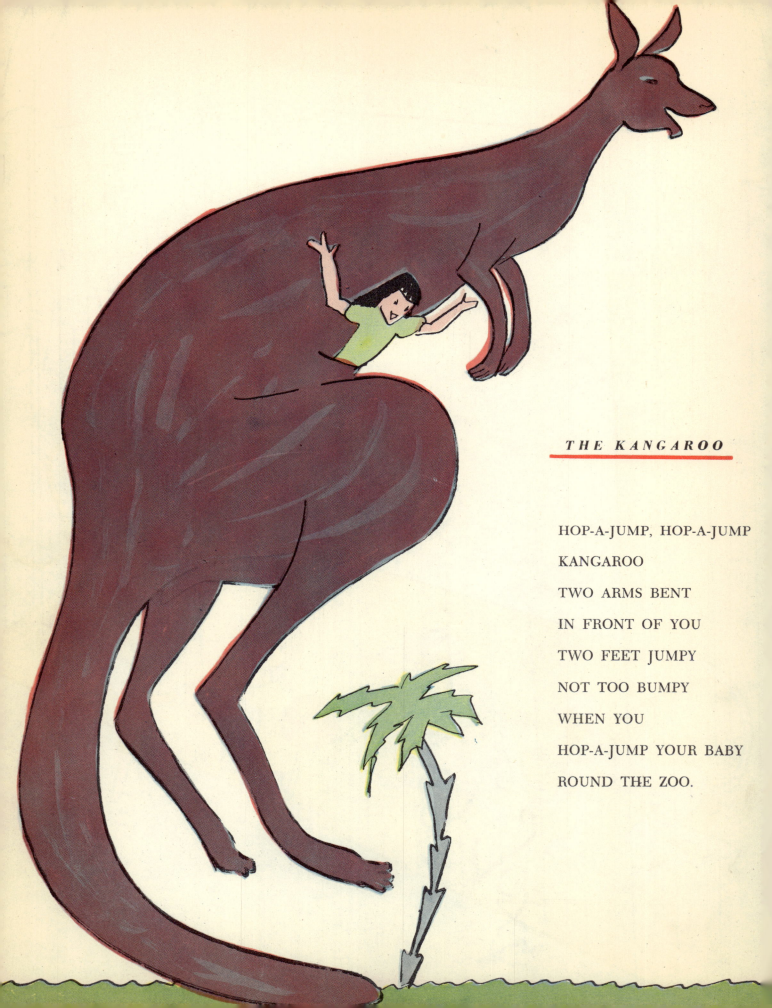

THE KANGAROO

HOP-A-JUMP, HOP-A-JUMP

KANGAROO

TWO ARMS BENT

IN FRONT OF YOU

TWO FEET JUMPY

NOT TOO BUMPY

WHEN YOU

HOP-A-JUMP YOUR BABY

ROUND THE ZOO.

THE KANGAROO

LYRICS BY MARION ABESON

MUSIC BY CHARITY BAILEY

Jumpy

I WON-DER WHY A KAN-GA-ROO GOES HOP! HOP! HOP! LUCK-Y THING SHE

SMOOTH

NEV-ER GOES HOP! HOP! FLOP! FOR SHE HAS A LIT-TLE FLAP. IT'S A

POCK-ET IN HER LAP, WHERE SHE KEEPS HER CO-ZY BA-BY SNUG AND WARM

THE SHINY BLACK SEAL

LYRICS BY MARION ABESON

MUSIC BY CHARITY BAILEY

Medium Slow

THE SHIN-Y BLACK SEAL LIFTS HER CHEST VER-Y HIGH TO CATCH A SIL-VER FISH AS IT GOES FLASH-ING BY. THEN SHE WAD-DLES, "FLAP! FLAP!" TO THE EDGE OF THE POOL AND DIVES WITH A "PLOP!" AND SHE FEELS SO NICE AND COOL.

KIND OF LIKE A BARK

SORT OF LIKE A SQUEAL

THAT'S HOW WE SING

LIKE A HUNGRY SEAL.

LOOK! NO HANDS —

NO FORK — NO DISH:

YOU OPEN YOUR MOUTH

AND YOU CATCH A FISH.

THE MONKEY

MONKEY SEE
MONKEY DO
WE CAN PLAY
LIKE MONKEYS
TOO:
FUNNY ME!
FUNNY YOU!

THE MONKEY

LYRICS BY MARION ABESON
MUSIC BY CHARITY BAILEY

Bouncy

THE MON-KEY EATS BA-NA-NAS LIKE YOU AND ME.___ HE CAN

SWING BY HIS ARMS AND CAN CLIMB UP A TREE.___ HE SCRATCH-ES "HIS-SELF"___ AND HE

WALKS ON ALL FOURS.___CAN HE DO A FAN-CY DANCE? WHY, YES. OF COURSE!

THE ELEPHANT

IS BIG AND LUMPY,

THE ELEPHANT

IS SLOW AND GRUNTY.

WITH HANDS TOGETHER

AND ARMS WAY DOWN

SWING THE SWINGIEST

TRUNK IN TOWN.

THE RUMBLY ELEPHANT

LYRICS BY MARION ABESON
MUSIC BY CHARITY BAILEY

DANCING IN THE KITCHEN

COME DANCE WITH ME
IN THE KITCHEN
CATCH A FISH
TO FRY.
CLIMB THE APPLE TREE
AND
SING A SONG OF APPLE PIE.
LET'S
LOOK AT MICHIE BANJO
STRUT:
HE'S SUCH A SILLY SIGHT!
WE'LL ASK MAMA
IF WE MAY DANCE
AND
STAY UP LATE TONIGHT.

IF THERE'S NO ONE AROUND
TO DANCE WITH YOU
DANCE AROUND YOURSELF —
MAKE BELIEVE YOU DO.

PLAY
LIKE A MONKEY ON A VIOLIN
WRIGGLE
LIKE A FISH IN A FRYING PAN
ROLL RIGHT OVER
WHEN YOU THINK YOU'RE DONE
THIS IS A SONG
THAT'S JUST FOR FUN.

SPRINKLE SPRINKLE PEPPER
AND DANCE WITH ME
BEST LITTLE DANCER
I EVER DID SEE.

NICE LITTLE FISH
IN A FRYING PAN
SIZZLE AND SHAKE
AS HARD AS YOU CAN.
CHOP-A-CHOP THOSE ONIONS
BUT DON'T YOU CRY,
YOU'LL EAT FISH SAUCE
BYE AND BYE.

COME DANCE WITH ME

LYRICS, *Based on the Creole,*
BY MARION ABESON

Creole Folk Tune
ARRANGED BY CHARITY BAILEY

SING A SONG OF APPLE PIE

LYRICS BY MARION ABESON

MUSIC BY CHARITY BAILEY

SING A SONG
OF APPLE PIE

LOTS OF LITTLE APPLES
A-HANGING ON THE TREE,
LET'S SHAKE DOWN THESE APPLES
MAKE A PIE FOR YOU AND ME.

CLEMENTINE'S A-COOKING,
MAYBE — BYE AND BYE —
IF WE BRING IN THOSE APPLES
SHE'LL MAKE AN APPLE PIE.

LOOK AT MICHIE BANJO

ONCE THERE WAS
A VERY FUNNY LITTLE FELLOW,
"BANJO" WAS HIS NAME.
EVERYBODY CALLED HIM
"LITTLE MICHIE BANJO."
HE ALWAYS LOOKED THE SAME.

HE ALWAYS HAD
A CIGAR IN HIS MOUTH
AS HE STRUTTED DOWN THE STREET.
SUCH A SILLY SHOW-OFF
LITTLE MICHIE BANJO
STRUTTING DOWN THE STREET.

YOU LOOK FUNNY, TOO,
WHEN YOU STRUT LIKE MICHIE BANJO
DOING A FUNNY WALK
WITH FUNNY FEET.

YOU LOOK *VERY* FUNNY
WITH THAT SILLY "CEEGAR,"
STRUTTING DOWN THE STREET!

LOOK AT MICHIE BANJO

Lyrics, *Based on the Creole,*
BY MARION ABESON

Creole Folk Tune
ARRANGED BY CHARITY BAILEY

LOOK AT MICH-IE BAN-JO, COCK-Y LIT-TLE FEL-LOW; STRUT-TING DOWN THE STREET.

DER - BY O - VER ONE EYE, MICH-IE BAN-JO; TWIRL-ING A YEL-LOW CANE.

SHIN - Y SHOES THAT GO "SQUEAK SQUEAK", MICH-IE BAN-JO; SMOK-ING A FAT "CEE-GAR."

LOOK AT MICH-IE BAN-JO, COCK-Y LIT-TLE FEL-LOW STRUT-TING DOWN THE STREET.

SOFTER

VERY SOFT

STRUT-TING DOWN THE STREET; STRUT-TING DOWN THE STREET.

THERE'S GOING TO BE
A BIG DANCE AT OUR HOUSE —
A DANCE THAT'S SO FANCY
THEY CALL IT A BALL:
WITH BEAUTIFUL LADIES
IN VELVET AND SILK
AND THE GENTLEMEN
HANDSOME AND TALL.

IF WE PROMISE TO BE
VERY QUIET AND GOOD
PERHAPS WE CAN PEEP
FROM THE HALL,
AND EAT ICE CREAM AND CAKE
AND STAY UP VERY LATE
AND WATCH THEM ALL
DANCE AT THE BALL.

WE'LL ASK MAMA

Creole Folk Tune
ARRANGED BY CHARITY BAILEY

LYRICS BY MARION ABESON

Light and Gay

WE'LL ASK MA- MA, DEAR.___ WELL ASK PA- PA, DEAR.___ TO LET US
I'LL BOW TO YOU, DEAR.___ YOU'LL BOW TO ME, DEAR.___ WE'LL SCRAPE THE

STAY AND WATCH THE LA-DIES DANC-ING AT THE BALL. IF MA-MA SAYS
BOWL AND LICK THE SPOON. AND HEAR THE FID-DLES PLAY. I'LL DANCE___WITH

"YES," DEAR.___ AND PA-PA SAYS "YES," DEAR.___ THEN WE WILL
YOU, DEAR.___ YOU'LL DANCE___WITH ME, DEAR.___ WE'LL DANCE AND

STAY AND WATCH THE LA-DIES DANC-ING AT THE BALL.
DANCE AND DANCE AND DANCE UN-TIL THE BREAK OF DAY.

MISTER PIG IN THE PAIL

STAY AWAY FROM MY POT,

JUMP BACK, LITTLE TOAD,

FIRE BURNS HOT.

SILLY COUSIN BAA SHEEP

YOU MADE MY LAMBIE CRY,

LITTLE GRAY MOUSE

YOU RUN AWAY —

BABY, HUSH-A-BYE.

MAMA   SAYS   "BE   CAREFUL"

WHEN MAMA SAYS "BE CAREFUL"
DON'T YOU FUSS AND CRY.
SING AND PLAY THESE LITTLE SONGS
AND HAVE FUN LEARNING WHY.

SILLY LITTLE JOHNNY

IT'S NO USE TO LIE —

A BOY WHOSE TONGUE IS PURPLE

ATE BLUEBERRY PIE.

DON'T TRY TO FOOL YOUR MAMA,

WHAT'S BEEN DONE IS DONE.

THE PIG CAUGHT IN THE DINNER PAIL,

COULD HE FOOL ANYONE?

MISTER PIG IN THE PAIL

LYRICS BY MARION ABESON

MUSIC BY MARION ABESON
ARRANGED BY CHARITY BAILEY

JUMP BACK, LITTLE TOAD

YOU'LL GET WARM BY JUMPING
WHENEVER YOU'RE FROZEN.
DON'T GO NEAR THAT FIRE
AND PUT YOUR COLD TOES IN.

JUMP BACK, LITTLE TOAD

LYRICS BY MARION ABESON   MUSIC BY CHARITY BAILEY

SILLY COUSIN BAA SHEEP

Based on a Southern Folk Song

LYRICS BY MARION ABESON

MUSIC BY CHARITY BAILEY

"MOTHER BAA BAA SHEEP,"
COUSIN BEGGED ONE DAY,
"LET ME TAKE YOUR LAMBIE
OUT WITH ME TO PLAY."

MOTHER BAA BAA SHEEP
LET HER LAMBIE GO.
MOTHER BAA BAA SHEEP
SHOULD HAVE ANSWERED "NO."

LITTLE GRAY MOUSE

SHUSH, MY BABY'S TIRED,
BABY WANTS TO SLEEP.
DON'T YOU BOTHER BABY,
DON'T YOU MAKE A PEEP.

POSTSCRIPT FOR PARENTS AND TEACHERS
FROM
A PARENT AND A TEACHER

The usual foreword for a book of this kind has been omitted because we wanted the songs to be enjoyed without preliminary direction or discussion. Though there is much commendable concern about the teaching of "music appreciation," young children do not need to be *taught* to appreciate music any more than they need to be *taught* to appreciate play. Children *feel* music with ever-growing pleasure from the time they are first able to hear any rhythmic sound, word pattern or melody. What children need for their happy development is suitable and attractive material with which to play and build as they grow. Children, like all of us, do best and learn most from that which they *love* to do.

The songs chosen for *Playtime With Music* have consistently pleased the children, parents and teachers who have heard them on records, at concerts and at school. They were written out of love for children and recognition of their dramatic and rhythmic needs and tastes.

The music arrangements are simple enough to be played by a child or an adult with limited training. Because children enjoy playing songs they know and can sing with their friends at school and play, this book will prove useful for early piano instruction. Its use should remove the "practise period" from its isolated and sometimes grimly "cultural" sphere.

Since these songs were first used, children have responded to them physically and imaginatively. They have had fun singing and acting them out and have made up wonderful dances to them. The introductory verses and the pictures which accompany the songs in this book spontaneously invite a child to play them out. Now many more parents, teachers and other people who work and play with children can use them. This makes us very happy indeed.

MARION ABESON
CHARITY BAILEY

4-1484